Where Is
Arizona?

Where Is Arizona?

by Jennifer Marino Walters

illustrated by Ted Hammond

Penguin Workshop

To Aunt Terry and Uncle A:
Thank you for featuring my books
prominently on your bookshelf!—JMW

PENGUIN WORKSHOP
An imprint of Penguin Random House LLC
1745 Broadway, New York, NY 10019
penguinrandomhouse.com

Designed and Produced by Dinardo Design, LLC.

Library of Congress Cataloging-in-Publication Data is available.

First published in the United States of America by Penguin Workshop, 2026

Manufactured in the United States of America
CJKW

ISBN 9798217053407 (paperback)
10 9 8 7 6 5 4 3 2 1

ISBN 9798217053414 (library binding)
10 9 8 7 6 5 4 3 2 1

The authorized representative in the EU for product safety and compliance is Penguin Random House Ireland, Morrison Chambers, 32 Nassau Street, Dublin D02 YH68, Ireland, https://eu-contact.penguin.ie.

Contents

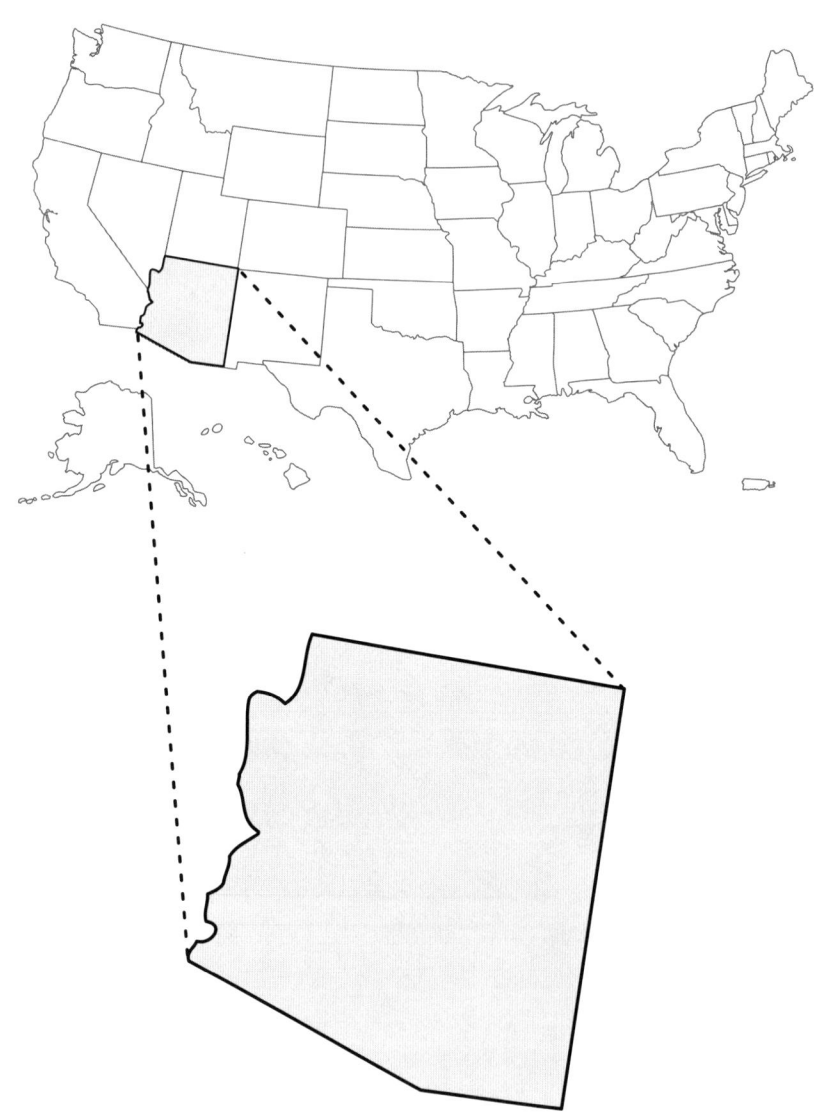

Where Is Arizona?

The year was 1903. President Theodore Roosevelt was taking a three-month journey through the American Southwest aboard a special train. On the morning of May 6, the president arrived in what is now Arizona. It was the first time he had ever been to the area. That's when he saw a breathtaking sight—the Grand Canyon.

The Grand Canyon is a deep, massive valley with steep rock sides in northwest Arizona. Twisting and turning for 278 miles, it features layers of rock in all sorts of colors, such as red, orange, golden brown, and pink. Roosevelt was overwhelmed by the views from the canyon's rim, or edge.

Before he left, Roosevelt made a now-famous speech to the crowd that had gathered. "Keep this great wonder of nature as it now is," he said. "You cannot improve on it. . . . What you can do is to keep it for your children, your children's children, and for all who come after you, as one of the great sights which every American . . . should see."

After Roosevelt left, the image of the Grand Canyon remained vivid in his mind, and his desire to protect it grew stronger. In 1908, he declared the Grand Canyon a national monument. But it wasn't until 1919 that the Grand Canyon finally got the full protection Roosevelt had dreamed of. On February 26 of that year, President Woodrow Wilson passed a law making the Grand Canyon the country's fifteenth national park. A national park is a special wilderness area protected by the US government.

Today, the Grand Canyon is the third most-visited of the sixty-three US national parks. Nearly five million people visit it each year! The Grand Canyon is also considered one of the seven natural wonders of the world. Carved out over millions of years by the mighty Colorado River, the world-famous canyon and the river that made it shaped much of Arizona's landscape.

CHAPTER 1
Arizona's Land and Environment

Arizona is in the southwestern United States. It is bordered by California to the west, Nevada to the northwest, Utah to the north, Colorado to the northeast, New Mexico to the east, and the country of Mexico to the south. The spot where Arizona, Utah, Colorado, and New Mexico meet is called the Four Corners Monument. If someone lies down and spreads their arms and legs, they can be in four states at once!

Arizona is the sixth-largest US state by land area and the fourteenth most populous state. Its capital, Phoenix (say: FEE-niks), is in the south-central part of Arizona. Phoenix is the most populous state capital in the United States.

The landscape in Arizona is full of contrasts.

Snowcapped mountains tower above lush green trees. Rivers run between deep, colorfully striped canyons. Beige, sandy desert areas are dotted with green cacti. More than half of Arizona has an elevation of four thousand feet or more, and a little over one quarter of the state is covered in forests.

The northeastern part of Arizona is the Colorado Plateau (say: plah-TOH). This area is full of flat-topped mountains called plateaus, mesas (hills with flat tops and steep sides), cliffs, and deep canyons.

The most famous and magnificent of these canyons is the Grand Canyon. It is six thousand feet deep at its deepest point—that's more than a mile—and eighteen miles across at its widest. To a person standing at the canyon's rim, a huge boulder at the bottom of the canyon would look like a tiny rock. The Grand Canyon can even be seen from outer space! Astronauts on the

International Space Station often take photos of it.

Most scientists believe the Grand Canyon is around 6 million years old. But the canyon's rock layers are much, much older. The youngest rock, near the top of the canyon, is 270 million years old. The oldest, at the bottom, is over 1.8 billion years old! These rock layers are different

colors, making the canyon walls look striped. But there's more to the Grand Canyon than just rock formations. It's home to more than seventeen hundred plant species, including cacti, yucca, agave plants, and many more.

Nearly 450 bird species, over 90 mammal species, and more than 40 reptile species also live at the Grand Canyon. The Grand Canyon

rattlesnake—a pink, venomous snake that can grow to over four feet long—is found nowhere else in the world. Another animal found only at the Grand Canyon is the Kaibab (say: KIE-bab) squirrel, a light gray squirrel with a black belly, a white tail, and long ears. Elk, porcupines, geckos, and bats are just a few of the other animals that call the canyon home. Visitors can hike or ride mules into and along the Grand Canyon and take rafting trips along the Colorado River. Some people even camp at the bottom of the canyon!

The Grand Canyon doesn't have the only impressive rock formations on Arizona's Colorado Plateau. North-central Arizona is known as Red Rock Country because of its red sandstone cliffs and giant red sandstone spires (tall, narrow, pointed rocks). The city of Sedona is part of Red Rock Country. So is Slide Rock State Park, a popular tourist spot with an eighty-foot natural water slide. Arizona's highest point, Humphreys

Peak, is also on the Colorado Plateau. Part of the San Francisco Mountains, the peak is 12,633 feet tall.

One of the world's best-preserved meteorite impact sites (places where a piece of rock or metal has fallen to Earth from outer space) is in northern Arizona, too. Meteor Crater (also known as the Barringer Crater) is a huge hole that's 570 feet deep and almost one mile wide. It was formed fifty thousand years ago when an iron asteroid (a small piece of rock that circles around the sun) crashed into Earth.

Northeast Arizona is home to Petrified Forest National Park, named for the many tree fossils found there. The tree logs washed into a river system over two hundred million years ago and were buried by sediment (material such as sand or stone that is deposited by water, wind, or glaciers). Minerals were absorbed into tiny openings in the wood over hundreds of thousands of years and replaced the wood's cells. The minerals eventually hardened into quartz, with a rainbow of colors that sparkle in the sunlight. Other crystals such as clear quartz and amethyst formed in cracks in the wood. Petrified Forest National Park is part of the Painted Desert, which features miles and miles of colorful, horizontally striped stone.

Running for over two hundred miles along the southwestern edge of the Colorado Plateau is the Mogollon (say: mah-guh-YOHN) Rim, a huge escarpment (a long cliff that separates two flat areas). The escarpment reaches as high as eight thousand feet, while the land south of the Mogollon Rim is at least one mile high.

Below the Colorado Plateau, stretching from northwest Arizona to the southeast part of the state, is the Transition Zone. This zone marks the transition from the forested highlands of the Colorado Plateau to the low deserts of southern Arizona's Basin and Range region. The Transition

Zone has elements of both regions.

The Basin and Range region makes up the western and southern third of Arizona. It's full of large, open-ended basins (areas of land that are lower than the area around them) and gently sloping valleys. These basins and valleys are broken up by parallel mountain ranges that

generally run in a north-to-south direction. Most of the people in Arizona live in the Basin and Range region.

The southern half of Arizona is largely part of the Sonoran Desert. The desert is the landscape that the state is perhaps best known for!

The Mighty Saguaro

The Sonoran Desert is famous for the saguaro (say: sah-WAH-roh) cacti that grow throughout it. The saguaro is the largest cactus in the United States. Cacti are a family of plants that usually have sharp spines or scales instead of leaves and have succulent stems built to hold water inside them. Saguaros grow to an average of forty feet tall—about the size of a three-story building. The tallest saguaro ever measured was seventy-eight feet tall! It grew about thirty miles north of Phoenix before toppling in a windstorm in 1986.

The saguaro can grow up to thirty inches in diameter (the distance through the center of something from one side to the other). Its root system can extend as far as one hundred feet. That's the length of a basketball court!

Saguaros often have multiple upturned arms, or branches. These arms usually begin growing when the saguaro is fifty years old or older. The arms are important because they absorb and store rainwater. The waxy exterior of the cactus keeps the water inside, where the plant can use it to survive desert heat.

Saguaros can live two hundred years or more. They are covered in gray pointy spines that protect them from thirsty animals and the hot sun. From late spring through early summer, saguaros produce white flowers, which were named the Arizona state flower in 1931.

The world's largest concentration of saguaro cacti is in southeastern Arizona's Saguaro National Park, within the Sonoran Desert. The park has roughly two million saguaro cacti!

The saguaro is one of nearly four thousand plant species that grow in Arizona. Trees such as pines, firs, spruces, and junipers grow in the forests, most of which are in northern Arizona. The world's largest stand (group of trees growing close together) of ponderosa pine trees stretches roughly 2.5 million acres along the Mogollon Rim. Arizona's deserts are full of cacti, mesquite trees, and shrubs such as sagebrush.

With southern Arizona being a desert, it has extremely hot summers and mild winters. The average high temperature in Phoenix, for example, is 106 degrees Fahrenheit in July! Northern Arizona has more moderate summer temperatures and cool to cold winters. Some parts get a lot of snow. Northern Arizona's largest city, Flagstaff, sits at an elevation of nearly seven thousand feet at the base of the San Francisco Peaks. Flagstaff is a snowy city, with over one hundred inches of snow per year on average.

The varying landscapes and climates in Arizona make for a diverse range of animal life. The state's forests are home to bears, mountain lions, elk, deer, and more. Bighorn sheep roam the rocky cliffs. Desert tortoises, scorpions, and Gila (say: HEE-luh) monsters live in the hottest, driest parts of Arizona. The Gila monster is one of only two lizard species in the world that are venomous (their bite is poisonous) to humans. Wild pigs called javelinas (say: have-uh-LEE-nuhs) roam throughout the state. Hawks, hummingbirds, and California condors are just a few of Arizona's many bird species. They've shared the land that is now Arizona with humans for a long time.

CHAPTER 2
State Origins

Scientists believe humans first lived in what we now call Arizona over twenty-five thousand years ago. These first peoples, known as Paleo-Indians, lived in caves and hunted animals (many of which no longer exist, such as mammoths and mastodons). The Cochise (say: KOH-cheese) culture likely began around ten thousand years ago and lasted until about 500 BCE. The Cochise focused less on hunting and more on gathering wild plants for food.

The Hopi (say: HOH-pee) people, one of the oldest living cultures, moved to present-day Arizona in the 1100s from Mexico, South America, and Central America. They set up villages of flat-roofed homes called pueblos in

northeastern Arizona. The multilevel pueblos were made of sun-baked clay called adobe (say: uh-DOH-bee) and stone. Each floor was set back from the floor below it, and people used wooden ladders to move between them. Many of these pueblos still exist as part of the Hopi Reservation, which includes twelve villages on three mesas— First Mesa, Second Mesa, and Third Mesa.

The Apache (say: uh-PAH-chee) and Navajo (say: NAH-vuh-hoh) peoples likely arrived in the area between 1100 and 1500 CE. They are believed to have traveled south from what is now western Canada and Alaska. The Apache lived in east-central and southeastern Arizona, while the Navajo settled near the Hopi in northeastern Arizona.

The Spanish began to explore this area in the 1530s. In 1540, Francisco Vázquez de Coronado (say: fran-SIS-ko vás-KEZ DEH core-uh-NAH-doh) led a large group of explorers to Arizona to try to claim the present-day American Southwest for Spain. They thought they'd discover cities full of gold and wanted to take resources from the land back to their home country. They found Hopi pueblo villages and the people who lived there. Members of Coronado's group became the first Europeans to see the Grand Canyon and the Colorado River.

More Spanish explorers came in the 1600s. They set up Catholic missions (places to teach or do the work of the church) in what is now northeastern Arizona in 1629. These missions tried to force Indigenous people into Christianity and the Spanish way of life, but many Indigenous people resisted. In 1680, a group of Pueblo people destroyed the missions.

The Spanish set up other missions after that, but many of those failed, too. Throughout the late 1600s and 1700s, the Spanish also fought with the Navajo people and other Indigenous groups over food and land.

Mexico gained independence from Spain in 1821 and took control of present-day Arizona. At the time, Arizona was part of Mexico's territory of Nueva California (New California), also called Alta California (Upper California). After the Mexican-American War (1846 to 1848), the United States gained control of the area that included what we call Arizona. Arizona became part of the Territory of New Mexico in 1850.

Until this time, very few Americans (other than explorers, soldiers, sheep drivers, and animal trappers) ventured into Arizona. But in 1851, the US Army sent groups of soldiers into Arizona to find a route for a wagon road to California. The Indigenous peoples resisted this takeover of their land. So, the US government began to set up army posts along the route.

Copper mining began in Arizona in 1854, in a town called Ajo (say: AH-hoh). Many more copper mines opened after that, including on the banks of the Colorado River and in central, eastern, and southeastern Arizona. That meant more people began moving to Arizona to work in the mines. They took over further Indigenous lands and met resistance from the people who already lived there.

Many Black people began moving to Arizona

around this time. Married couple Wiley and Hannah DuPont Box are believed to be the first Black settlers in Tucson. They moved there between 1850 and 1855 and worked different jobs, including mining. More Black people followed and created a strong community in the desert.

These Black people moved to Arizona of their own free will. There were very few enslaved Black people there, mostly because Arizona's economy did not rely on plantations (large farms), where many enslaved people in the southern states lived and worked. Still, slavery was not officially banned in Arizona until 1863.

On February 24, 1863, the western half of the New Mexico Territory became the Territory of Arizona. That year, Lieutenant Colonel (say: lew-TEN-ent KER-null) Christopher "Kit" Carson launched a bloody war against the Apache people in New Mexico and the Navajo Nation in New

Mexico and Arizona. The US Army began to forcibly remove the Apache and the Navajo from their homelands.

In an event known as the Long Walk, which began in 1864, nearly nine thousand Navajo people were forced to leave their homes in northwestern New Mexico and northeastern Arizona and march three hundred miles to a reservation (an area of land kept separate as a place for Indigenous peoples to live) in eastern New Mexico called the Bosque (say: BAHSK) Redondo Reservation. They were to join about five hundred Apache people who'd already been forced to move. Hundreds of Navajo people died along the way due to starvation and illness. Those who did make it to the reservation faced harsh living conditions, disease, and more starvation. Over three thousand more died. The Apache and Navajo people living at the reservation were also forced to assimilate (take on the ways of a

different culture) to white culture, though many continued to resist.

In 1868, things changed for the Navajo. The US government and the Navajo Nation signed a treaty, the US-Navajo Treaty of 1868, that allowed them to return to a part of their homeland and set up a reservation. The reservation covered 3.4 million acres in northeastern Arizona and northwestern New Mexico. But part of that area

included land that Hopi people were living on.
This sparked years of disputes with the Hopi
Nation over land rights.

In 1877, a man named Ed Schieffelin (say:
SHEF-lin) discovered silver in southeast Arizona.
He set up a silver mine there and named it, and the
area surrounding it, Tombstone. (People had told
him he'd find nothing there but his tombstone.)
Once word got out about Schieffelin's discovery,

people rushed to Tombstone to find their own silver. By 1881, about seven thousand people had moved there. It had become one of the richest mining towns in the Southwest. Tombstone was a classic Wild West town, marked by lawlessness, violence, and crime. Cowboys, criminals, and pioneers who came to build new lives often fought for control.

Wyatt Earp (say: UHRP) and his two brothers were lawmen in Tombstone. The Earps and their friend Doc Holliday often fought with two sets of brothers, cowboys Billy and Ike Clanton and Tom and Frank McLaury. The feud ended in 1881 with a gun battle between the two groups at a horse enclosure called the O.K. Corral. Billy Clanton and the two McLaury brothers were killed. Wyatt Earp escaped without injury. The gun battle only lasted thirty seconds, but its legend lives on. Many movies have been made about it. The O.K. Corral is now a tourist spot where visitors can immerse themselves in the Wild West and experience a reenactment of the gunfight.

As mining increased in the 1870s, some people also tried to set up farms along Arizona's rivers and streams. Droughts (say: DROWTS) and floods made it very difficult. That's when plans began for flood-control and water-storage systems.

In 1911, the Salt River Project was completed. This project delivered water to farmers near Phoenix. Farming improved, and bigger cities sprang up around the area. But Arizona still experienced many water shortages as its population increased.

CHAPTER 3
Growth and Development

On February 14, 1912, Arizona officially became the forty-eighth US state. Only Alaska and Hawaii are newer. Its population increased quickly. The state became known as the place of the five Cs—copper, cattle, cotton, citrus, and climate. That's because those were the biggest parts of Arizona's economy and brought many people to the state. Arizona's clean, dry air and warm climate attracted people from the rest of the country.

Tourism began to increase, too. During the 1920s and 1930s, many dude ranches (vacation resorts where people can do typical cowboy activities such as horseback riding) opened in the state. They allowed guests to experience a

tourist version of the culture of the Old West. Many luxury hotels also opened during this time. They included two that are still open today—the Arizona Biltmore Hotel in Phoenix and the Wigwam Resort in Litchfield Park.

This left Arizona with a new challenge: How would it provide water to all those new residents and visitors? The state turned to its longest river—the mighty Colorado.

A Man-Made Marvel

For many years, the Colorado River was an unpredictable force in the American Southwest. It sometimes caused huge floods. When he became secretary of commerce in 1921, Herbert Hoover suggested building a dam on the Colorado River. The dam would prevent flooding, help irrigate (water) crops, and provide water to people living in the area.

Construction on the dam began in 1930 and was completed about five years later. During that time, over twenty thousand people worked on it.

Located on the state line between Arizona and Nevada, the Hoover Dam is as tall as a sixty-story building. Its base is as thick as the length of two football fields. The dam contains enough concrete to pave a road from San Francisco all the way to New York City.

Today, the Hoover Dam provides water to over sixteen million people and irrigates more than 1.5 million acres of land. Guests can ride an elevator nearly 530 feet into the bottom of the dam and tour passageways and tunnels.

The Hoover Dam dramatically changed the landscape of Arizona by controlling the flow of the Colorado River and creating Lake Mead. Due to long periods without rain and increased use of the water in the river, the amount has been decreasing. This has led to less power production in the dam, as well as concerns about future water shortages.

During World War II (1939 to 1945), several US military bases and flight schools opened in Arizona. So did German prisoner-of-war camps and Japanese American internment camps. During this war, the United States and its allies fought against the Axis powers, which included Germany and Japan.

From 1942 to 1945, many people of Japanese descent were forced to leave their homes. Even

though they were US citizens, many Japanese Americans were required to live in crowded camps called internment camps, which they weren't allowed to leave. Two of these internment camps were in Arizona—one near Phoenix and the other in southwestern Arizona. These camps did not provide enough food and living space. The people living in them had little privacy or comfort. When the war ended, the camps closed. Many Japanese

Americans returned to their communities, while some chose to go other places.

While the war continued in Europe, two large German prisoner-of-war camps were established in Arizona. They were Camp Papago Park in eastern Phoenix and Camp Florence in central Arizona. German soldiers who were captured during the war were taken to these camps. Those at Camp Papago Park were treated fairly well and generally given enough food and leisure time. When the war ended, most prisoners of war returned to Germany.

After World War II, Arizona's population exploded. This was due in part to the increased use of air-conditioning, which made Arizona's hot summers more bearable. The state attracted many retired or elderly people who wanted to escape the cold winters of the Midwest. Some of them moved to Arizona year-round, while others bought winter homes there.

All along, people worked hard to find a way to solve Arizona's water-shortage problem. This included a long fight with California over the use of the waters of the Colorado River. In 1963, the US Supreme Court granted Arizona the right to a portion of that water. Congress then authorized the Central Arizona Project in 1968, which allowed for a huge system of pumps and canals to carry water from the Colorado River to the areas around Phoenix and Tucson. That project was finished in 1993.

Indigenous nations in Arizona, including the Navajo, Hopi, and San Juan Southern Paiute (say: PIE-yoot) peoples, have been fighting for decades for their rights to water. In June 2024, the three nations finally approved an agreement with the state that would give them rights to the water from part of the Colorado River Basin. Congress failed to approve the deal, and the fight continues.

CHAPTER 4
Today's State

Today, about one quarter of Arizona is made up of reservations where Indigenous nations live. Twenty-two federally recognized Indigenous groups live on these reservations. The largest is the Navajo Nation, who refer to themselves as Dine, meaning "the people" (also the largest Indigenous group in the entire country). The Hopi, the Havasupai (say: hav-uh-soo-PYE), and the Hualapai (say: hoo-ah-lah-PYE) are other large Indigenous groups in Arizona. The Navajo and Hopi live in northeastern Arizona, where some Hopi people still live in pueblos. The Havasupai and Hualapai also live in the northern part of the state.

Arizona is one of the states with the highest

numbers of Indigenous language speakers. Navajo is the most commonly spoken Indigenous language in the United States. Hopi and Navajo paintings, pottery, baskets, and jewelry are also an important part of the arts in Arizona.

Groups of working artists live in Scottsdale, Sedona, Tucson, and Tubac. There are many

places in Arizona where people can see art on display. Phoenix's Heard Museum has a huge collection of Indigenous art. Indigenous arts and crafts can also be found at the Sharlot Hall Museum in Prescott, the Museum of Northern Arizona in Flagstaff, and other museums. At the Phoenix Art Museum, visitors can see Western American, Asian, Latin American, and European art along with fashion design.

The five Cs remain important parts of Arizona's economy. Arizona is still the top copper-producing state, responsible for about two-thirds of the copper produced in the country. Arizona is also a major cotton producer. Beef and dairy products come from Arizona cattle, and citrus fruits such as oranges, lemons, grapefruit, and tangerines are grown in the state.

Rodeos are a huge part of Arizona's culture. A rodeo is a competition that shows off skills such as bull riding and cattle roping. One of the

oldest professional rodeos in the country, Prescott Frontier Days, began in Prescott, Arizona, in 1888. The Tucson Rodeo includes over seven hundred cowboys and cowgirls.

Many people keep cool in Arizona by swimming, boating, fishing, and more in many of Arizona's numerous lakes (128 in total). A popular one is Lake Havasu in western Arizona. There, visitors can also see the London Bridge—yes, the actual one—which moved to Lake Havasu City

after city founder Robert McCulloch purchased it in 1968! The bridge had been built in 1831 to replace an older version. After the purchase, it was taken apart, moved to Arizona stone by stone, and reassembled across the Colorado River. It opened to the public in 1971.

Arizona has contributed to astronomy and our understanding of space. The Lowell Observatory in Flagstaff, established in 1894, has advanced telescopes and other equipment. It was there that

a man named Clyde Tombaugh (say: TOM-bo) discovered Pluto in 1930.

The University of Arizona in Tucson also has an important space program and observatory, the Steward Observatory. Researchers at the university played an important role in developing the Hubble Space Telescope. About the size of a large school bus, Hubble launched into space in 1990 and travels around Earth, taking pictures of planets, stars, and galaxies. In 1997, the Near Infrared Camera and Multi-Object Spectrometer (NICMOS) was added to Hubble. Created by University of Arizona researchers, the camera allowed the telescope to take more detailed pictures.

Several professional sports teams play in Arizona. These include the National Football League's Arizona Cardinals, the National Basketball Association's Phoenix Suns, Major League Baseball's (MLB) Arizona Diamondbacks, and the Women's National Basketball Association's Phoenix Mercury. Fifteen MLB teams also do their spring training in Arizona. And the state has hosted four Super Bowls, including in 2023, when the Kansas City Chiefs beat the Philadelphia Eagles in Super Bowl LVII at State Farm Stadium in Glendale.

Arizona is home to many golf courses, and large professional golf tournaments take place there. Auto racing is another big sport in the state. NASCAR hosts races each year at Phoenix Raceway in Avondale. And the state's deserts and forests draw thousands of campers, hunters, and hikers.

With red rocks, green cacti and forests, brown deserts, blue-green lakes, and more, Arizona is a rainbow of color that attracts new residents and visitors alike. Over forty-five million people visited Arizona in 2023, and that number keeps growing.

Arizona at a Glance

Statehood: 1912

Nickname: The Grand Canyon State

Abbreviation: AZ

State Motto: *Ditat Deus* (Latin for "God Enriches")

State Tree: Palo Verde

State Mammal: Ringtail

State Song: "Arizona March Song" and "Arizona"

Capital: Phoenix

Size: 113,990 square miles

Population: Over 7 million

Famous People from Arizona: Cesar Chavez (civil rights activist), Stevie Nicks (singer), Hailey Bieber (model), Linda Ronstadt (singer)

Phoenix ★

State flag

State flower
Blossom of the
saguaro cactus

State bird
Cactus wren

FUN FACT:

Arizona and Hawaii are the only two US states that do not observe Daylight Saving Time (DST). However, the Navajo Nation in northeast Arizona does observe DST.

Timeline of Arizona

1100s — The Hopi move to what is now Arizona

1629 — The Spanish set up Catholic missions in what is now northeastern Arizona

1680 — A group of Pueblo people destroy the Spanish missions

1864 — The Navajo are forced to move to the Bosque Redondo Reservation and endure the Long Walk

1868 — The US-Navajo Treaty allows the Navajo to return to part of their lands in Arizona and New Mexico

1881 — Wyatt Earp and Doc Holliday are involved in a notorious gun battle at the O.K. Corral in Tombstone

1888 — One of the country's first professional rodeos begins in Prescott

1912 — Arizona becomes the forty-eighth US state

1919 — The Grand Canyon becomes a US national park

1930 — Construction begins on the Hoover Dam

1971 — The London Bridge debuts in Lake Havasu City

1993 — The Central Arizona Project is completed, carrying water from the Colorado River to the Phoenix and Tucson areas

2023 — Super Bowl LVII takes place at State Farm Stadium in Glendale

Timeline of the World

1163	Work begins on the Notre Dame Cathedral in Paris, France
1543	Polish astronomer Nicolaus Copernicus publishes his theory that Earth revolves around the sun
1564	William Shakespeare is baptized
1660	Charles II becomes king of Great Britain and Ireland
1867	The United States buys the Alaska Territory from Russia
1881	Clara Barton establishes the American Red Cross
1886	German engineer Karl Benz demonstrates the first gas-powered car
1903	The Wright brothers make the first powered airplane flight in Kitty Hawk, North Carolina
1914	The Panama Canal is completed, linking the Atlantic and Pacific Oceans
1919	Jackie Robinson is born
1935	The board game Monopoly goes on sale for the first time
1977	*Star Wars* opens in movie theaters
1993	The World Wide Web becomes available to the public
2022	The Argentina national football team wins the FIFA World Cup

Bibliography

*Books for young readers

*Gregory, Josh. *Arizona*. A True Book: My United States. New York: Scholastic Children's Press, 2018.

*Hirsch, Rebecca E. *What's Great About Arizona?* Minneapolis: Lerner Publishing Group, 2015.

*Mattern, Joanne. *The Grand Canyon: This Place Rocks*. South Egremont, MA: Red Chair Press, 2018.

*O'Connor, Jim. *Where Is the Grand Canyon?* New York: Penguin Workshop, 2015.

Websites

Grand Canyon: www.nps.gov/grca/index.htm

Hopi Nation: www.hopi-nsn.gov

Navajo Nation: www.navajo-nsn.gov